Spiritual Disciplines
Journal

Is the Spiritual Disciplines Journal right for me?

Do you struggle each morning or evening remembering to be grateful for your blessings in life? Have you heard you should have some kind of a journaling practice, but just don't know where to start? Is it difficult for you to find the time to serve and help others? Do you feel as though you're sometimes floundering in life without a clear, defined purpose?

Enter the Spiritual Disciplines Journal.

Each day begins with an inspirational Bible verse and a clear call to gratitude, along with identifying one person you can serve or pray for that day. This will help you grow spiritually, systematize a practice of gratefulness, and remember to take time out of your day to serve others. Each day ends with self-examination and a review of your purpose statement, allowing you to identify what you have done well, what you could have done better, and how connected you are to your life's purpose.

Whether you are simply interested in Christianity and the spiritual disciplines, a brand new Christian, a long-time follower of Christ and spiritual devotee, a Bible study leader, a parent, a student, a child or anyone else who wants to experience the power of gratitude, service, self-examination and purpose, you'll find everything you need in the Spiritual Disciplines Journal.

My name is Ben Greenfield and I'd like to welcome you to the Spiritual Disciplines Journal.

As an author, speaker and consultant in the realms of health, fitness, nutrition and body and brain optimization, I'm perhaps most well-known for my teachings on biohacking, fitness, muscle gain, fat loss, nutrition, supplements, longevity, cognition and beyond. But for much of my life, I did not focus upon building my spiritual muscles in the same way that I prioritized physical disciplines such as caring for my metabolic health, growing my physical muscles, or tending to the neurons in my brain.

However, after years of pursuing body and brain optimization, I grew to realize that the relatively self-obsessed or carnal pursuits of a lower body fat percentage, finding the perfect diet, climbing your own personal Mount Everest of a triathlon, Spartan race, or CrossFit competition, learning a host of new languages and musical instruments, increasing the health of your blood and biomarkers or "reversing the aging process" are all ultimately unfulfilling, and can often leave one standing at the top of the mountain of physical and mental achievement, yet feeling disappointed and extremely empty inside despite having accomplished what might appear to the world to be lofty and admirable goals.

Most of us inherently know that caring for our soul is important, but we somehow shove it to the side because, let's face it: life gets busy and it just seems far more practical and immediately useful to go hit the gym rather than sitting cross-legged on the floor meditating and praying, spending an extra five minutes in bed in the morning gratitude journaling, or prioritizing relationships during a long and joyful family dinner. Fact is, I personally spent about 20 years of my life, up until I was in my mid-30's, barely tending to my spirit—until I realized that my own unhappiness and constant striving for the next big physical, mental, business and personal achievement and obstacle to overcome was simply leaving my spirit even more shriveled, shrunken, unfit and neglected, and leaving me unfulfilled, unhappy and unable to fully love others and to make a maximum, purpose-filled impact with my life for God's glory.

Over the past several years, as I have repeatedly witnessed in both myself and others the ultimate unfulfillment of a sole focus upon carnal, fleshly pursuits, and as I've observed great thinkers and philosophers while continually seeking for and asking for God's wisdom, I've become increasingly convinced that caring for one's spirit is as important—no, actually far more important, than caring for one's body and brain. After your muscles have atrophied, your skin has sagged, your brain has degraded and accumulated with plaque, your blood vessels have become clogged, and your nerves have become weakened—long after your relentless pursuit of fitness or health or longevity has become a vain effort—your spirit can be just as strong and as bright as ever. Perhaps nowhere is this "soul importance" more eloquently stated than in Matthew 16:26: *"For what profit is it to a man if he gains the whole world, and loses his own soul?"* Yet sadly, it seems that the spirit is the most oft-neglected component of our human vessels, and that's often due to an ignorance of the spiritual disciplines, or the failure to systematize and prioritize these disciplines into our daily routine.

So what do I mean by the spiritual disciplines?

Spiritual disciplines are specific habits that develop, grow, and strengthen our spirit, that build the muscles of our character, and that train our soul. You can consider them to be the barbells, dumbbells, weight training machines and running trails of our inner being. In his book *Spiritual Disciplines For The Christian Life,* Donald Whitney succinctly defines the spiritual disciplines as those practices found in Scripture that promote spiritual growth among believers in the gospel of Jesus Christ, and specifically focuses upon Bible intake, prayer, worship, evangelism, serving, stewardship, fasting, silence, solitude, journaling and learning. Another book that I own, the *Spiritual Disciplines Handbook* by Adele Ahlberg Calhoun, contains seventy-five different spiritual disciplines, including well-known practices such as gratitude, meditation, singing, worship, and relationships, along with more fringe and lesser known habits such as pilgrimages, retreats, mentoring, centering prayer and care of the earth (incidentally, I spent nearly two years taking my family through Adele's book by visiting, discussing and implementing a new spiritual discipline once every two weeks!).

Why is a regular practice of the spiritual disciplines so important? It's quite simple, really: in the same way that mental muscles must be repeatedly challenged to enable your brain to stay young, grow new neurons and constantly develop and expand, and in the same way that physical muscles must be repeatedly stressed to stay strong, grow new fibers and constantly become more mobile and functional, the spiritual muscles must be consistently trained to be able to experience sustained, productive growth, expansion and enlightenment. This takes structure, direction and discipline, which involves more than simply taking a peek at the Bible each morning, saying a quick prayer as you drive your car to work or ducking into church once a week on Sunday morning. While these tiny habits aren't bad per se, they certainly are not going to transform you into a truly disciplined spiritual warrior who can impact others in a deep and meaningful way, into a well-rounded disciple prepared and equipped to defend the hope that is within you, or into a warrior for God who can withstand the fiery darts of the evil one and the constant temptation that knocks upon the door of your heart each day. In other words, the spiritual disciplines keep you from becoming spiritually unfit, spiritually bereft and spiritually stagnant. Nobody ever became supremely intelligent by reading Curious George books their entire life, nor did anyone ever become supremely fit by hoisting a dumbbell over their head one time each week.

Does this mean that by disciplining ourselves spiritually, we can toil and sweat our way into heaven with good works? Hardly. The spiritual disciplines are not a way to earn our way into heaven, but are instead a means by which we are fully able to experience and enjoy the fruits of the Holy Spirit and to fully receive the grace of God that sanctifies and saves us. As Richard J. Foster writes in his excellent book *Celebration of Discipline*:

> " *The Disciplines allow us to place ourselves before God so that he can transform us...God has ordained the Disciplines of the spiritual life as the means by which we place ourselves where he can bless us.* "

When you begin to implement and systematize the spiritual disciplines into your own life, you'll discover that your entire existence becomes more meaningful and more purposeful. You'll experience a deep and rich satisfaction that outlasts any runner's high or exercise endorphin release you might get from a physical workout. You'll find yourself in a constant, joyful union with God each day, and radiating a distinct peace and hope that others around you sense, feel and even ask you about.

You are now holding in your hands the key to unlocking powerful spiritual disciplines that I have implemented in my own life, and that I'm now blessed to be able to share with you: gratitude, service, self-examination and purpose. While all the spiritual disciplines are important, these four disciplines are those I've found to be most precious and meaningful for me and my family, and quite appropriate for habitually weaving into one's daily routine: gratitude, service, self-examination and purpose.

Let's begin with the first spiritual discipline that is a core element of each morning entry in your journal: gratitude.

Gratitude

In studying the writings and teachings of Dr. Robert Emmons, who I consider to be the world's leading authority on gratitude, I've discovered that throughout history, gratitude has been categorized as an emotion, an attitude, a moral virtue, a habit, a personality trait, and a coping response. The word gratitude itself is derived from the Latin root gratia, which means grace, graciousness, or gratefulness, and all derivatives from this Latin root seem to relate to kindness, generosity, gifts, the beauty of giving and receiving, or the feeling you've gotten "something for nothing."

This means that the object of gratitude is other-directed and that gratitude stems from the perception of a positive personal outcome that is neither deserved or earned and due to the actions of another person. According to Emmons, gratitude results from a two-step process: 1) recognizing that one has obtained a positive outcome, and 2) recognizing that there is an external source for this positive outcome.

The benefits of gratitude are impressive indeed. Let's first consider the physical benefits of this powerful spiritual discipline. Research has shown that grateful people experience fewer aches and pains and they also report feeling healthier than other people. Not surprisingly, grateful people are also far more likely to take care of their health. They exercise more often and are more likely to attend regular check-ups with their doctors - not because they are sick, but because they have a greater sense of self-awareness and actually care about their bodies.

Sure: some of this can possibly be attributed to the fact that those who are feeling better physically might tend to be more thankful and happy - but this is not always the case. As a matter of fact, studies have shown that when people actively take the time to list the things they are grateful for, they feel far better mentally and physically than participants of the same health status who haven't done the same. In other words, gratitude's physical benefits are not only correlational, but in many cases causal.

Research also shows that when we simply think about what we are grateful for, the parasympathetic, rest-and-digest, calming component of the nervous system is triggered, producing a host of positive benefits for the body, including decreasing stress-associated cortisol levels and increasing oxytocin, which is a powerful bonding and "feel-good" hormone.

Studies have also shown that people who are more grateful have better heart health, less inflammation and healthier heart rhythms, and that gratitude can ward off depression, stress and anxiety, which are all associated with increased risk of heart disease. As a matter of fact, when researchers have performed blood tests for inflammation and plaque buildup in the arteries, they have discovered significantly lower levels among those who had a gratitude practice!

A gratitude practice also helps you sleep better, which has a significant impact on physical health and overall daily function. Multiple studies have shown that those who express gratitude more often sleep better and longer, that writing in a gratitude journal significantly improves sleep quality and that gratitude helps improve quality of sleep and lowers blood pressure.

Gratitude has a significant impact on psychological health too, and reduces not only symptoms of depression, but also a multitude of toxic emotions ranging from envy and resentment to frustration and regret - all while simultaneously increasing levels of overall happiness and life satisfaction! Gratitude also improves mental resilience. For example, research has shown gratitude not only reduces stress, but it also plays a major role in overcoming trauma and post-traumatic stress disorder. This means that being aware of all you have to be thankful for - even during the worst times of your life - fosters an intense resilience that helps you battle stress and get through tough times.

From a psychological standpoint, gratitude can also act as a natural antidepressant. When we take the time to consider what we are grateful for, specific neural circuits are activated that result in increased production of dopamine and serotonin, and these neurotransmitters then travel through neural pathways to the "bliss" center of the brain - similar to the mechanisms of many antidepressants. Gratitude also increases blood flow to and activity in the hypothalamus, the brain section that controls release of feel-good hormones such as oxytocin, which elicits a positive effect both physically and psychologically.

Fascinatingly, it appears that along with these psychological benefits, gratitude can literally rewire your brain (in a good way). For example, one brain-scanning study demonstrated that even months after a simple, short gratitude writing task, the human brain remains "rewired" to feel extra thankful, with significantly increased activity in the frontal, parietal, and occipital regions of the brain, particularly when a participant gave a gift, or received a gift. Increased sensitivity to other's feelings and emotions was also observed in the pregenual anterior cingulate, a section of the brain involved in both empathy and in predicting the effects of one's own actions on other people. The results from these and other brain-scanning studies suggest that the more practice you can give your brain at feeling and expressing gratitude, the more it actually adapts to this mind-set, meaning you can think of your brain as having an actual gratitude "muscle" that can be exercised and strengthened. This also means that the more effort you make to feel gratitude in the present, the more the feeling of gratitude will come to you spontaneously in the future.

This data also helps explain another established finding: that gratitude can create a positive feedback loop. In other words, the more thankful you feel, the more likely you are to be empathetic, to understand others, and to act pro-socially toward others, which can then cause them to feel grateful and set up a positive cascade that is highly related to the fact that our emotions and beliefs can affect not only our own mind and body, but the mind and body of those around us (a topic addressed quite thoroughly in books such as Bruce Lipton's *Biology Of Belief* or Dawson Church's *Mind Over Matter*).

The Bible also teaches that the expression of gratitude is incredibly important. Colossians 3:17 says, *"And whatever you do in word or deed, do all in the name of the Lord Jesus, giving thanks to God the Father through Him,"* and Ephesians 5:20 says, *"Thanks always for all things to God the Father in the name of our Lord Jesus Christ."*

Paul opens his letters to the Romans, Ephesians, Philippians, Colossians, both the Thessalonians, 2 Timothy and Philemon with clear gratitude by thanking God and expressing gratefulness for the churches to which he is writing.

But even when we understand the actual power of gratitude, the deep, primal physical and psychological roots we seem to have tied to this emotion, and even the commandments from the Bible to be thankful in all, it's often too tempting to shove a gratitude practice to the side and instead prioritize rushing, achieving, worrying, complaining, grumbling and engaging in every other aspect of life that seems to easily distract us from simply stopping to be grateful. I guarantee that the very best antidote for this common resistance to remember to be grateful is a structured gratitude practice in which you are not simply saying "thank you" to the bank teller or supermarket employee, not only breathing a quick prayer of gratefulness over breakfast, and not smiling and waving at someone who allows you to merge ahead of them in traffic, but instead to have a daily spiritual discipline of actually writing down one thing that you are grateful for, each and every day of the year.

This is exactly why very first question you will answer each day in your Spiritual Disciplines Journal is based on gratitude:

"What am I grateful for today?"

Here is how I recommend you go about answering this question and beginning your first Spiritual Disciplines Journal entry. Keep this journal with a pen or pencil nearby right by your bedside so that gratitude is one of your first impulses when you wake. Let this be the first impulse when you wake up. Along with your Bible, let the this journal hold a coveted spot on your bedside dresser, just an arm's reach away. Within a few days, the habit will become automatic. To begin your gratitude practice, wake up, take a deep breath, close your eyes and dwell on a positive experience from the day before, the night before, or even that morning. Do this as you're lying in bed or perhaps sitting in your favorite chair in your bedroom. As you take a deep breath and close your eyes, ask yourself, "What am I grateful for?" You'll often find it is the simplest of things: the birds you hear outside, the sunlight streaming through the window, the pitter-patter of a child's foot going up or down stairs, the soft skin of your lover in bed next to you, or simply the refreshed feeling of having experienced a solid night's rest. Then, simply write down what it is that first comes to your mind.

Sometimes, things can be a bit more difficult: you don't have a great night of sleep, you wake up with the sniffles, your phone is blowing up with texts, or it's a dark, stormy day outside. This is where the magic of gratefulness takes over because you're suddenly forced to find the silver lining in any situation. For example, two nights ago, I woke up groggy, having gotten just four hours of sleep. The day was cloudy, my wife was out of town with the kids, and I felt less than stellar. But as I took a deep breath and closed my eyes, I realized how grateful I was for the ability to breathe. As I filled my lungs with oxygen, I felt a surge of gratitude for something as simple as being able to take in air through my nose and my mouth. And what did I write down?

"I am grateful for fresh air, the breath of life, and the wonderful complexity of my lungs."

See? It's that easy! Within just a few days, this habit - along with the other three spiritual disciplines you're about to discover - will become automatic.

Service

Service is a spiritual discipline that allows you to help others in a spirit of love, sacrifice, empathy, charity and goodwill for your fellow humans. In his book *The Spirit of the Disciplines*, Dallas Willard describes service this way:

> " *In service we engage our goods and strength in the active promotion of the good of others and the causes of God in our world. Here we recall an import-*

ant distinction. Not every act that may be done as a discipline need be done as a discipline. I will often be able to serve another simply as an act of love and righteousness, without regard to how it may enhance my abilities to follow Christ ...But I may also serve another to train myself away from arrogance, possessiveness, envy, resentment, or covetousness. In that case, my service is undertaken as a discipline for the spiritual life. "

This means that in a way, the practice of service achieves two goals: both helping others, and also enabling us to take our focus off ourselves and the all-too-common positive daily affirmations of "I'm good, I'm great, I'm wonderful, and gosh-darn-it, people like me!" and instead move through life in a spirit of unselfishness and a focus upon the Golden Rule - loving our neighbors as ourselves and doing unto others as we would have them do unto us.

In his book *Celebration of Discipline*, Richard Foster lists activities that fall under the category of the discipline of service, including:

Hospitality: showing hospitality to one another without grumbling and cheerfully sharing our home with those who may need a meal or a place to stay.

- Listening: loving God by listening to His Word and His still small voice in the silence, and also learning to love others by listening to them with no shame or judgement.

- Bearing others' burdens: empathizing with one another's hurts and sufferings, weeping with those who weep, and helping others cast their burden, sorrows and pain upon Jesus.

- Spreading the good news of the Gospel to others: sharing the reason for the love, hope and joy that is within us so that others can experience the same peace and transformation.

In Luke 22:27, Jesus said: *"I am among you as the one who serves."* Committing ourselves to serving others in full presence, love and humility, just as Jesus did, without seeking any reward other than glorifying God, is indeed a lofty discipline worth making a habit in our lives, don't you think?

Consider a few other examples from the myriad of verses within the Bible about service:

Galatians 5:14
"For all the law is fulfilled in one word, even in this:
"You shall love your neighbor as yourself."

Acts 20:35
"And remember the words of the Lord Jesus, that He said,
'It is more blessed to give than to receive.'"

Matthew 10:42
"And whoever gives one of these little ones only a cup of cold
water in the name of a disciple, assuredly,
I say to you, he shall by no means lose his reward."

This is why, each morning in your Spiritual Disciplines Journal, you'll answer the following question:

"Who can I pray for or serve this day?"

As you ponder the answer to this question each morning, I encourage you to spark your imagination with reflective questions such as:

What can I do to make the world a little brighter today, to use my skills and talents to make a difference? Do I know someone that needs encouragement or support? Is there a way to use my skills and unique gifts to contribute meaningfully to the world in a way that satisfies my life's purpose? What random act of kindness can do today? When you set the intention every day to be of service in a clear, specific way, you'll find your self examination at the end of each day becomes even more meaningful and inspiring. You will feel a deep, rewarding sense of inner peace and joy when you review any selfless accomplishments at the end of the day.

You'll also find that the more you engage in service, the more opportunities for service God will bring your way. You will discover yourself meeting more neighbors, inviting old and new friends over for dinner, volunteering in and connecting more to your local community, engaging in deeper relationships with your loved ones, and approaching your entire day with a refreshing, unselfish attitude.

You may have noticed that this particular question - *"Who can I pray for or serve this day?"* - presents you with the option to not only serve others physically, but to pray for others too.

Why? There are two reasons. First, when the Lord has placed someone on your heart for you to help, you can certainly take action and do good deeds for that person, but the power of prayer means that you can also pray for that person for a potent "one-two combo" of making a positive impact in the life of someone else and also reaching out to God to bestow His presence upon that person's life. Second, suppose the person who you are inspired to help that day is somewhere across the country or across the world. You may not be able to physically help them mow their lawn or fill their moving van or eat a home-cooked meal - but you can certainly pray for that person! The simple act of praying for someone God has placed upon your heart is certainly an act of service in and of itself.

Here are a few personal examples of how you can reply to this question in your journal:

When I found out that my dear friend Matt who lives two states away was experiencing a tough time in his relationship with his wife, I wrote down:

"Matt." It's that simple! Because of that simple note, I was inspired the rest of the day to pray for him.

Another time, I rolled over and looked at my wife lying there next to me. I was not only overwhelmed with a feeling of gratitude about how much she accomplishes for our household and our family, but also overwhelmed with the desire to really "be there for her" that day. So it was her name that I jotted down in my journal, and it was her that I went out of my way to both pray for and serve the rest of the day.

When I realized that our annual church program to feed children at a local poverty-stricken elementary school was kicking off, I wrote down the name of the school principal and said a prayer for him. Later that day I gave him a phone call to see if there was anything I could help with to get the program moving along - all steps I probably would have neglected to take if I had not begun my day with a spirit of service!

As you implement this discipline, service will become a natural part of your life. In the years I spent prior to developing this habit, I noticed a distinct lack of service in my busy, day-to-day routine. Sure, I read my Bible, prayed, had excellent health, took care of my family, and lived what appeared to be a happy and successful life. However, there was a glaring absence of attention to the world's needs for food and water, a lack of humble willingness to go meet and serve my neighbors and volunteer for charity work in my community. Now that I start every day by listing one person I can pray for or serve, I've grown into a far less selfish and far more aware, selfless, and serving person. As you journal each day, you'll experience the same edifying transformation.

Having established the understanding and importance of beginning each day by refreshing our spirits with both gratitude and service, let's now turn from the morning habit of your spiritual discipline journaling to the evening habits within the Spiritual Disciplines Journal.

Self-Examination

I first became familiar with the daily practice of self-examination when reading a biography of Benjamin Franklin, and later studying his *Book Of Virtues*, in which he describes his own journaling system for focusing upon 13 specific daily virtues ranging from patience to honesty to smart spending. As a part of this system, Franklin created his own process of self-examination as a way to cultivate his "passion for virtue" and his focus upon continual moral improvement. In the morning, he would ask himself: "What good shall I do this day?" Then in the evening, he would reflect upon his daily routine by asking himself: "What good have I done today?"

Years later, while bringing my family through Adele Calhoun's *Spiritual Disciplines Handbook*, I became re-familiarized with this evening practice of self-examination, in which Calhoun encourage us to ask questions such as:

When today did I have the deepest sense of connection with God, others, and myself? When today did I have the least sense of connection?

What was the most life-giving part of my day? What was the most life-thwarting part of my day?

Where was I aware of living out of the fruit of the Spirit? Where was there an absence of the fruit of the Spirit?

What activity gave me the greatest high? Which one made me feel low?

It turns out this spiritual discipline of self-examination - also known as the "Examen" - can be traced in origin back to the ancient philosophers of Greece and Rome, with one of earliest iterations found in the Golden

Verses of Pythagoras, which reads:

> " Do not welcome sleep upon your soft eyes before you have reviewed each of the day's deeds three times:
>
> 'Where have I transgressed?
> What have I accomplished?
> What duty have I neglected?' "

Beginning from the first one go through them in detail, and then, If you have brought about worthless things, reprimand yourself, but if you have achieved good things, be glad."

Later, the Stoic philosopher Seneca wrote of the Roman philosopher Quintus Sextius:

> " This was Sextius's practice: when the day was spent and he had retired to his night's rest, he asked his mind:
>
> Which of your ills did you heal today?
> Which vice did you resist?
> In what aspect are you better?
>
> Your anger will cease and become more controllable if it knows that every day it must come before a judge . . .
>
> I exercise this jurisdiction daily and plead my case before myself. When the light has been removed and my wife has fallen silent, aware of this habit that's now mine, I examine my entire day and go back over what I've done and said, hiding nothing from myself, passing nothing by. "

The Bible also contains many verses that encourage a process of self-examination and laying one's deeds for the day out before God, including 1 Corinthians 11:28: *"But a man must examine himself, and in so doing he is to eat of the bread and drink of the cup."*; Psalm 139:24: *"And see if there be any hurtful way in me, and lead me in the everlasting way."*; Psalm 139:23: *"Search me, O God, and know my heart; try me and know my anxious thoughts."*; Job 13:23: *"How many are my iniquities and sins? Make known to me my rebellion and my sin."*; and Psalm 26:2: *"Examine me, O Lord, and try me; test my mind and my heart."*

This is why each evening, you will follow in the path of Benjamin Franklin, along with these ancient Stoics, philosophers, religious leaders, and Scriptural teachings and answer the following two questions in your Spiritual Disciplines Journal:

"What good have I done today?"

"What could I have done better today?"

When I first began this evening process of self-examination, I was surprised at the results, and I suspect you will be too. While I often end a day with a general sense of whether the day went poorly or the day went well, until I actually began to examine my thoughts and actions for the day, I found I never really understood why I was peaceful or stressed, joyful or melancholy, and focused or scattered. By beginning to take the time to review everything I did, felt and experienced for the day, I was able to begin identifying when I was using my time well and when I wasn't, whether I had set up schedules and habits that allowed for deeper union with God and others and whether I hadn't, and what type of practices, mood states and situations or environments allowed me to live out my life's purpose in full presence and selfless love, and which didn't. Each day transformed from a confusing and difficult-to-decode blur to a clear and meaningful twenty-four hour learning experience.

As you experience the same transformation, you will begin to identify patterns in your daily routine that can be changed for the better, habits that should be kept and habits that should be halted, and even people who drain your energy and people who fill you with peace, love and joy. You'll discover those things you should have accomplished yet didn't, and those things you may have perhaps wasted your time on that you can avoid in the future. Did you rush mindlessly through each meal without nary a thought of the blessing and wonder of God's creation of food? Did you skip a workout to spend an extra hour at the office, or did you take time for self-care and self-love? Did you spend much of your day in reactive and draining rather than productive and energizing tasks? Was your screentime and consumption inordinately high relative to your productivity and creation? Were you fully present or distracted and absent in your conversations?

When paired with a morning discipline of gratitude and service, and the final spiritual discipline of purpose that you are about to discover, your evening practice of self-examination will be physically, mentally and spiritually transformative, and, through incremental improvements, will make you a more impactful individual who never ends a day feeling as though you're wasting your time or not living out the full purpose for your life.

Purpose

The Okinawans refer to purpose as *ikigai* (translated as "reason for being") and Nicoyans as *plan de vida* ("reason to live"). Interestingly, these regions are both known as "Blue Zones," or longevity hotspots with a disporporaintely high number of centenarians, or people over the age of 100 years who still live healthy, active, productive, robust and purposeful lives.

Research has indeed proven that people who know their life and have a clear purpose for which they wake each morning live longer lives. One 11-year long study that investigated the correlation between having a sense of purpose and longevity showed that those who expressed having a clear purpose in life lived longer than those who did not and also stayed immersed in activities and communities that allowed them to be involved in fulfilling that purpose.

I recommend you not only know your purpose in life, but also that you be able to state it in one succinct sentence.

So how exactly does one identify their purpose in life? *I've studied up on this quite a bit, and there are plenty of purpose-finding materials and resources I've thoroughly read and reviewed, with some of my favorites including:*

- *Claim Your Power* by Mastin Kipp
- *Limitless* by Jim Kwik
- *Personality Isn't Permanent* by Benjamin Hardy
- *The Values Factor* by John DiMartini
- *Don't Waste Your Life* by John Piper
- *True North: Discover Your Authentic Leadership* by Bill George
- Websites such as **Life Purpose Quiz**, **TheWhyStack.com**, **StartWithWhy.com**, and **WhyInstitute.com**

So do you now need to drop everything and spend the next three months of your life reviewing all those resources? Maybe. You'd probably come out the other side a better, more purposeful person.

But one area in which I think I can do you a convenient service is to succinctly distill into a few key tips what I personally learned from each of these books and websites, and what I see as recurring themes in most purpose-finding literature and resources like those cited above. I can guarantee that if you use the following steps and tips I've created to identify your purpose, you'll have harnessed 80% of the goodness from those resources above and be left with the option to delve into them on your own free time, if you so desire.

As you read the steps below, I recommend you take distraction-free time to jot down your replies with a pen or pencil and paper, then use the specially designated section at the end of this Spiritual Disciplines Journal introduction to write your completed purpose statement.

PURPOSE-FINDING STEP 1
What did you like to do when you were a kid?

You were born with a unique set of skills and talents—things you tend to be good at based on the way your brain is wired, the way your genetics are assembled, and the way your body is built. As a result of these nature-based traits, along with nurture-based influence from the family and households you grew up in, you likely tend to enjoy and be good at specific activities.

For example, I grew up absolutely loving reading books; writing stories; learning via documentaries, courses, and movies; teaching what I learned to others; singing songs; speaking in front of people; creating art and new ideas; and competing in sports and other games, such as chess and video games.

So my own personal purpose statement is…

> …*"To Read & Write, Learn & Teach, Sing & Speak, Compete & Create In Full Presence & Selfless Love, To The Glory Of God."*

See how that weaves in many of the same things that made me excited when I was a kid? Those are the activities that still ignite my joy and put me into a state of flow.

If you're a bit foggy about what you were actually like and what you enjoyed to do when you were a little boy or a little girl, then, if your parents or relatives who were close to you at that time are still alive, invite those folks out to dinner or a coffee. When you sit down with them, ask them one question:

"What was I like when I was a kid?"

That's it. Then prepare to sit back, listen, and take notes.

PURPOSE-FINDING STEP 2
What puts you "in the zone" now?

In positive psychology, a flow state, also known as "being in the zone," is a mental state in which you are performing an activity where you are fully immersed in a feeling of energized focus, full involvement, enjoyment, and presence in the process of that activity.

For example, if I sit down in front of a blank Word document on my computer and begin to write, my concept of time vanishes. I'll write for hours. Words just *flow* out of me. I don't think about food or drink, and I'm often oblivious to everything else going on around me, even if I'm in a busy coffee shop. I've always been wired that way. My wife, on the other hand, absolutely detests writing and would rather walk on a bed of nails than pen an essay. However, if you plant her in front of a blank canvas and give her a set of paintbrushes and oil, she'll absolutely bloom, painting for hours on end as she enters the zone with a satisfied smile on her face. (I, on the other hand, will cringe as I forcefully attempt to "make art happen.")

So what puts you in the zone at this point in your life? Writing? Art? Craftsmanship like woodworking or building something with your hands? Gardening? Exercise? Programming?
Identify those activities, and weave them into your purpose statement. I

guarantee you'll find overlap between those activities and what you enjoyed doing when you were a kid.

PURPOSE-FINDING STEP 3
What naturally comes easy to you?

This may seem a bit redundant with what you enjoyed doing when you were a kid and what puts you in the zone now, but it's important to take into account because if your purpose statement is built around those activities that naturally come easy to you, you'll be highly self-actualized as you live out that purpose statement. Self-actualized people are those who are significantly fulfilled, driven, and joyful in their day-to-day activities. For self-actualized people living out their true purpose in life, a day of work often feels like a day of play.

And guess what? There's absolutely nothing to be ashamed about if work comes easy to you. Often, we have a belief pattern, perhaps influenced by the traditional so-called Puritanical work ethic philosophy* that a day of work needs to be a day of drudge, drenched in blood, sweat, and tears; and we frequently believe that only at the end of a day of work can we take a deep sigh of relief and "play" (although we're typically so exhausted by the hard work that play is the equivalent of junk food binges, video games, and Netflix).

But, as Mark Twain said, if you *"find a job you enjoy doing, you will never have to work a day in your life."*

Others have shared Twain's thoughts. Here's what Stephen King has to say:

> " *Yes, I've made a great deal of dough from my fiction, but I never set a single word down on paper with the thought of being paid for it… I have written because it fulfilled me.*

*Maybe it paid off the mortgage on the house and got the kids through college, but those things were on the side–I did it for the buzz.
I did it for the pure joy of the thing.
And if you can do it for the joy, you can do it forever.* "

Steve Jobs noted that:

" *Your work is going to fill a large part of your life, and the only way to be truly satisfied is to do what you believe is great work. And the only way to do great work is to love what you do.* "

Then there's Thomas Edison, who said:

" *I never did a day's work in my life, it was all fun.* "

You get the idea. Work can just *flow* from you. When it does, and when it feels like play, that's another sign you're living out your true purpose. Sure, there will be times when you experience what Steven Pressfield refers to as the "resistance"—rationalizing, fear and anxiety, distractions, the voice of an inner critic, and other elements that keep you from creating your authentic art, whatever that creation of art might be—but this resistance doesn't indicate you're not living out your purpose. It's just the day-to-day temptation towards laziness or fear of the unknown, failure, or embarrassment that we all face. Learn to identify the resistance to living your purpose, embrace the resistance as a sign that you're engaged in something impactful, then press on (and definitely read Pressfield's book *Do The Work!*).

*a quick note regarding the Puritanical work ethic. I don't mean to throw the Puritans under the bus. In the book, "Exploring New England's Spiritual Heritage," *author Garth Rosell describes how the Puritans were encouraged to identify their purpose in life with much prayer and reflection, to take into account their natural gifts and inclinations, to seek the advice and confirmation their friends and family, and to consider the practical needs of the community in which they lived. Interestingly, those who were gifted for and inclined to "sundry callings" (the equivalent of a blue-collar worker, such as farming, construction, etc. – which in modern days could be the warehouse worker, firefighter, construction worker, custodian, etc.) must seek to discover which of these callings is "the best." Similarly, those who were privileged to study in what was called "the schools of the prophets" and at liberty to become school-masters, physicians, lawyers, or ministers were considered to have a special obligation to seek among these available options their very "best calling."*

Regardless of what career was chosen by these Puritans, their callings were encouraged to conform to three basic principles. First, to serve the public good and to seek one another's welfare. Second, to have "gifts of body and mind" suitable to that calling (although they also believed rightly that when God calls a person to a particular task, he will also provide the appropriate gifts to fulfill it). Third, to be sure that calling is from God, by relying upon prayer, the guidance of the Bible, the counsel of friends, the encouragement of the community and the existence of an open door opportunity.

If that vocation was considered to be homely, boring or ordinary, they focused upon performing that task nonetheless to the glory of God and the good of others. After all, Jesus himself girded himself with a towel, and washed His disciples' feet. If a Puritan was anxious about whether or not their work was successful, they were encouraged to "cast their burden upon the Lord" and to find contentment whatever the circumstance.

So ultimately, while I don't think that work, especially working in our true purpose and calling, needs to be viewed as a daily drudge of sweat, blood and tears, I do agree with this Puritan philosophy that no matter what your work is, it should be chosen carefully according to your unique gifts and the counsel of God, friends and family, be done in full excellence, with a spirit of love towards others with no complaining, and, finally should "multiple purposes" be available to one, the best purpose is the one most highly suited to your gifts.

PURPOSE-FINDING STEP 4
Summarize your purpose into one single, succinct statement that you can memorize.

This next step will take practice. Write down all those things you loved to do when you were a kid, those activities that put you into the flow now, and what naturally comes easy to you. Then connect the dots and try to express all those elements into one single, succinct purpose statement that you can easily memorize.

Again, my purpose statement is…

…*"To Read & Write, Learn & Teach, Sing & Speak, Compete & Create In Full Presence & Selfless Love, To The Glory Of God."*

Before that, it was…

…*"To Empower People To Live A More Adventurous, Joyful & Fulfilling Life".*

Keep your purpose statement specific, precise, concise, clear, and goal-oriented. Write it down. It might be two to three paragraphs at first. Then a paragraph. Then a couple of sentences. Then one sentence. Refine it. Edit it. Write it again. Have no guilt about changing it a dozen times if need be. But you must, must, must make it short and easy to memorize so that you can quickly recall it and rely upon it when the bullets of the matrix of life are flying at you and you need to remind yourself of why you are doing what you are doing.

Finally, understand that your purpose statement - like the two examples of my own previous and current purpose statement stated above - can change over time as your passions and personality changes. C.S. Lewis, one of my favorite authors of all time, once said *"You are never too old to set another goal or to dream a new dream."* So your purpose statement during this chapter of the book that is your life may change in the next chapter of your life. That's OK. Don't feel guilty, flaky, or schizophrenic about that. Be open to change and do so by sitting down with your purpose statement on at least a yearly basis—reviewing it, analyzing it, praying over it, meditating upon it, and questioning it to get clarity on whether it still fully aligns with what your soul knows to be true. Run it by friends and family members to get an objective opinion. Do that the first time you write your purpose statement and continue to do it for every future purpose statement you create.

PURPOSE-FINDING STEP 5
Love God & love others with your purpose.

Finally, no matter how good your purpose statement is, it will never be truly fulfilling or impactful if it's all about *you*. If the motivation behind and reason for your purpose statement is to make more money, own a better car, have a nicer home, attract successful people, run faster, get stronger or achieve, achieve, achieve, then you'll never truly be happy, and in the end, your purpose will feel selfish, meaningless, empty, and unfulfilling.

Instead, once you have written your purpose statement sentence, you must go forth and love others with your purpose. Bless others selflessly with your purpose. Change the world with your purpose because you love people, not because you want to fulfill Maslow's Hierarchy of Needs or scratch your own back. Follow the Golden Rule with your purpose. Pursue your purpose with zero selfishness and in full love for your fellow human beings, and, trust me, the rewards back to you will naturally come in due time. But the focus of living out your purpose statement should *not* be on your own happiness, but rather the happiness of others. That's what will truly make you happy.

Furthermore, don't just love others with your purpose, but also love God with your purpose. After all, you were created a unique being in the image of God, and one of the greatest things you can do with your purpose is to wake up each morning and, as one of my trusted mentors once told me, *"Do the very best thing that day with whatever God has put on your plate."* By doing your work and living out your purpose each day with supreme excellence, you'll magnify and glorify the mightiest Being this world knows, and that's the greatest love and greatest gift you can give back to the Creator who put you here in the first place and bestowed upon you the unique skills, body, and brain you've been blessed with.

One of my favorite preachers, John Piper, puts it this way:

> " *We are not called to be microscopes. We are called to be telescopes…*
> *There is nothing and nobody superior to God.*
> *And so the calling of those who love God is to make his greatness*
> *begin to look as great as it really is. That's why we exist, why we were saved,*
> *as Peter says in 1 Peter 2:9,*
>
> *"You are a chosen race, a royal priesthood, a holy nation, a people for his own possession, that you may proclaim the excellencies of him who called you out of darkness into his marvelous light.* "

So our whole duty in life, therefore, can be summed up like this: Feel, think, and act in a way that will make God look as great as he really is. Be a telescope for the world of the infinite starry wealth of the glory of God. Yes, live your purpose in full love for others and for the magnification and glory of God. I guarantee the impact of your life will be profound if that's the lens through which you see and manner with which you live out your purpose.

So now it's simply time to calendar a time, with your Spiritual Disciples Journal nearby, to address these thought exercises:

1. What did you like to do when you were a kid?
2. What puts you "in the zone" now?
3. What naturally comes easy to you?
4. Summarize your purpose into one single, succinct statement that you can memorize.
5. Love God & love others with your purpose.

Based on all this, as an integral part of your Spiritual Disciplines Journal, you must spend time over the next hours, day, week, or month identifying, honing, writing, and memorizing your purpose; and then, in the space below, write your purpose statement:

I _____, commit to writing in my Spiritual Disciplines Journal for at least 7 days in a row, starting __ / __ / __.

Writing in this journal is important to me because (e.g. deeper union with God, knowing myself better, making a greater impact with my life, etc.):

_____
_____
_____
_____
_____
_____
_____

If I finish 7 days of journaling, I will reward myself with (e.g. a trip to my favorite restaurant, a nice bottle of wine to share with friends, a long nature hike, etc.):

_____
_____

_____

_____

_____

_____

_____

_____

I will do the following to ensure I journal each day (e.g. keep the journal by my bedside with a pen handy, sharing my journal with someone I love for accountability, having a calendar I mark an X on for each day I journal, etc.)

_____

_____

_____

_____

_____

_____

_____

_____

Spiritual Disciplines
Journal

I have been young, and now am old; Yet I have not seen the righteous forsaken, Nor his descendants begging bread. He is ever merciful, and lends; And his descendants are blessed.

Psalms 37:25, 26

___ / ___ / ___

Morning

What am I grateful for today?

Who can I pray for or serve this day?

Evening

What good have I done today?

What could I have done better?

What is one way I lived my purpose statement today?

For the word of God is living and powerful, and sharper than any two-edged sword, piercing even to the division of soul and spirit, and of joints and marrow, and is a discerner of the thoughts and intents of the heart.

Hebrews 4:12

___ / ___ / ___

Morning

What am I grateful for today?

Who can I pray for or serve this day?

Evening

What good have I done today?

What could I have done better?

What is one way I lived my purpose statement today?

For God so loved the world that He gave His only begotten Son, that whoever believes in Him should not perish but have everlasting life.

__ / __ / __

John 3:16

Morning

What am I grateful for today?

Who can I pray for or serve this day?

Evening

What good have I done today?

What could I have done better?

What is one way I lived my purpose statement today?

Therefore, if anyone is in Christ, he is a new creation; old things have passed away; behold, all things have become new.

2 Corinthians 5:17

___ / ___ / ___

Morning

What am I grateful for today?

Who can I pray for or serve this day?

Evening

What good have I done today?

What could I have done better?

What is one way I lived my purpose statement today?

> *Stand therefore, having girded your waist with truth, having put on the breastplate of righteousness, and having shod your feet with the preparation of the gospel of peace; above all, taking the shield of faith with which you will be able to quench all the fiery darts of the wicked one. And take the helmet of salvation, and the sword of the Spirit, which is the word of God;*
>
> **Ephesians 6:14-17**

___ / ___ / ___

Morning

What am I grateful for today?

Who can I pray for or serve this day?

Evening

What good have I done today?

What could I have done better?

What is one way I lived my purpose statement today?

Therefore we also, since we are surrounded by so great a cloud of witnesses, let us lay aside every weight, and the sin which so easily ensnares us, and let us run with endurance the race that is set before us, looking unto Jesus, the author and finisher of our faith, who for the joy that was set before Him endured the cross, despising the shame, and has sat down at the right hand of the throne of God.

Hebrews 12:1, 2

___ / ___ / ___

Morning

What am I grateful for today?

Who can I pray for or serve this day?

Evening

What good have I done today?

What could I have done better?

What is one way I lived my purpose statement today?

Consider the lilies, how they grow: they neither toil nor spin; and yet I say to you, even Solomon in all his glory was not arrayed like one of these.

Luke 12:27

___ / ___ / ___

Morning

What am I grateful for today?

Who can I pray for or serve this day?

Evening

What good have I done today?

What could I have done better?

What is one way I lived my purpose statement today?

Casting all your care upon Him, for He cares for you.

1 Peter 5:7

___ / ___ / ___

Morning

What am I grateful for today?

Who can I pray for or serve this day?

Evening

What good have I done today?

What could I have done better?

What is one way I lived my purpose statement today?

And you shall love the Lord your God with all your heart, with all your soul, with all your mind, and with all your strength.' This is the first commandment. And the second, like it, is this: 'You shall love your neighbor as yourself.' There is no other commandment greater than these.

Mark 12:30-31

___ / ___ / ___

Morning

What am I grateful for today?

Who can I pray for or serve this day?

Evening

What good have I done today?

What could I have done better?

What is one way I lived my purpose statement today?

Honor your father and your mother, as the Lord your God has commanded you, that your days may be long, and that it may be well with you...

Deuteronomy 5:16

___ / ___ / ___

Morning

What am I grateful for today?

Who can I pray for or serve this day?

Evening

What good have I done today?

What could I have done better?

What is one way I lived my purpose statement today?

Let nothing be done through selfish ambition or conceit, but in lowliness of mind let each esteem others better than himself. Let each of you look out not only for his own interests, but also for the interests of others.

Philippians 2:3, 4

___ / ___ / ___

Morning

What am I grateful for today?

Who can I pray for or serve this day?

Evening

What good have I done today?

What could I have done better?

What is one way I lived my purpose statement today?

And whenever you stand praying, if you have anything against anyone, forgive him, that your Father in heaven may also forgive you your trespasses. But if you do not forgive, neither will your Father in heaven forgive your trespasses.

Mark 11:25, 26

___ / ___ / ___

Morning

What am I grateful for today?

Who can I pray for or serve this day?

Evening

What good have I done today?

What could I have done better?

What is one way I lived my purpose statement today?

So then, my beloved brethren, let every man be swift to hear, slow to speak, slow to wrath; for the wrath of man does not produce the righteousness of God.

James 1:19, 20

___ / ___ / ___

Morning

What am I grateful for today?

Who can I pray for or serve this day?

Evening

What good have I done today?

What could I have done better?

What is one way I lived my purpose statement today?

Let all bitterness, wrath, anger, clamor, and evil speaking be put away from you, with all malice. And be kind to one another, tenderhearted, forgiving one another, even as God in Christ forgave you.

Ephesians 4:31, 32

___ / ___ / ___

Morning

What am I grateful for today?

Who can I pray for or serve this day?

Evening

What good have I done today?

What could I have done better?

What is one way I lived my purpose statement today?

He will swallow up death forever, And the Lord God will wipe away tears from all faces; The rebuke of His people He will take away from all the earth; For the Lord has spoken.

Isaiah 25:8

___ / ___ / ___

Morning

What am I grateful for today?

Who can I pray for or serve this day?

Evening

What good have I done today?

What could I have done better?

What is one way I lived my purpose statement today?

Finally, brethren, whatever things are true, whatever things are noble, whatever things are just, whatever things are pure, whatever things are lovely, whatever things are of good report, if there is any virtue and if there is anything praiseworthy—meditate on these things. The things which you learned and received and heard and saw in me, these do, and the God of peace will be with you.
Philippians 4:8-9

___ / ___ / ___

Morning

What am I grateful for today?

Who can I pray for or serve this day?

Evening

What good have I done today?

What could I have done better?

What is one way I lived my purpose statement today?

*The grass withers, the flower fades,
But the word of our God stands forever.*

Isaiah 40:8

___ / ___ / ___

Morning

What am I grateful for today?

Who can I pray for or serve this day?

Evening

What good have I done today?

What could I have done better?

What is one way I lived my purpose statement today?

For to me, to live is Christ, and to die is gain.

___ / ___ / ___

Philippians 1:21

Morning

What am I grateful for today?

Who can I pray for or serve this day?

Evening

What good have I done today?

What could I have done better?

What is one way I lived my purpose statement today?

No temptation has overtaken you except such as is common to man; but God is faithful, who will not allow you to be tempted beyond what you are able, but with the temptation will also make the way of escape, that you may be able to bear it.
1 Corinthians 10:13

___ / ___ / ___

Morning

What am I grateful for today?

Who can I pray for or serve this day?

Evening

What good have I done today?

What could I have done better?

What is one way I lived my purpose statement today?

A merry heart does good, like medicine,
But a broken spirit dries the bones.

___ / ___ / ___

Proverbs 17:22

Morning

What am I grateful for today?

Who can I pray for or serve this day?

Evening

What good have I done today?

What could I have done better?

What is one way I lived my purpose statement today?

Enter by the narrow gate; for wide is the gate and broad is the way that leads to destruction, and there are many who go in by it. Because narrow is the gate and difficult is the way which leads to life, and there are few who find it.

Matthew 7:13-14

___ / ___ / ___

Morning

What am I grateful for today?

Who can I pray for or serve this day?

Evening

What good have I done today?

What could I have done better?

What is one way I lived my purpose statement today?

For I know the thoughts that I think toward you, says the Lord, thoughts of peace and not of evil, to give you a future and a hope. Then you will call upon Me and go and pray to Me, and I will listen to you. And you will seek Me and find Me, when you search for Me with all your heart.
Jeremiah 29:11-13

___ / ___ / ___

Morning

What am I grateful for today?

Who can I pray for or serve this day?

Evening

What good have I done today?

What could I have done better?

What is one way I lived my purpose statement today?

If you then, being evil, know how to give good gifts to your children, how much more will your Father who is in heaven give good things to those who ask Him!

Matthew 7:11

___ / ___ / ___

Morning

What am I grateful for today?

Who can I pray for or serve this day?

Evening

What good have I done today?

What could I have done better?

What is one way I lived my purpose statement today?

Be still, and know that I am God;
I will be exalted among the nations,
I will be exalted in the earth!

Psalms 46:10

___ / ___ / ___

Morning

What am I grateful for today?

Who can I pray for or serve this day?

Evening

What good have I done today?

What could I have done better?

What is one way I lived my purpose statement today?

He gives power to the weak, And to those who have no might He increases strength.

___ / ___ / ___

Isaiah 40:29

Morning

What am I grateful for today?

Who can I pray for or serve this day?

Evening

What good have I done today?

What could I have done better?

What is one way I lived my purpose statement today?

*Be of good courage, And He shall strengthen your heart,
All you who hope in the Lord.*

Psalms 31:24

___ / ___ / ___

Morning

What am I grateful for today?

Who can I pray for or serve this day?

Evening

What good have I done today?

What could I have done better?

What is one way I lived my purpose statement today?

> *Therefore do not worry, saying, 'What shall we eat?' or 'What shall we drink?' or 'What shall we wear?' For after all these things the Gentiles seek. For your heavenly Father knows that you need all these things.*
>
> **Matthew 6:31, 32**

___ / ___ / ___

Morning

What am I grateful for today?

Who can I pray for or serve this day?

Evening

What good have I done today?

What could I have done better?

What is one way I lived my purpose statement today?

Now faith is the substance of things hoped for, the evidence of things not seen.

Hebrews 11:1

___ / ___ / ___

Morning

What am I grateful for today?

Who can I pray for or serve this day?

Evening

What good have I done today?

What could I have done better?

What is one way I lived my purpose statement today?

Let your conduct be without covetousness; be content with such things as you have. For He Himself has said, 'I will never leave you nor forsake you.'

Hebrews 13:5

___ / ___ / ___

Morning

What am I grateful for today?

Who can I pray for or serve this day?

Evening

What good have I done today?

What could I have done better?

What is one way I lived my purpose statement today?

Blessed is the man whom You instruct, O Lord, And teach out of Your law, That You may give him rest from the days of adversity, Until the pit is dug for the wicked.

Psalms 94:12, 13

___ / ___ / ___

Morning

What am I grateful for today?

Who can I pray for or serve this day?

Evening

What good have I done today?

What could I have done better?

What is one way I lived my purpose statement today?

> *But as many as received Him, to them He gave the right to become children of God, to those who believe in His name: who were born, not of blood, nor of the will of the flesh, nor of the will of man, but of God.*
>
> **John 1:12, 13**

___ / ___ / ___

Morning

What am I grateful for today?

Who can I pray for or serve this day?

Evening

What good have I done today?

What could I have done better?

What is one way I lived my purpose statement today?

Trust in the Lord, and do good; Dwell in the land, and feed on His faithfulness. Delight yourself also in the Lord, And He shall give you the desires of your heart. Commit your way to the Lord, Trust also in Him, And He shall bring it to pass.

Psalms 37:3-5

___ / ___ / ___

Morning

What am I grateful for today?

Who can I pray for or serve this day?

Evening

What good have I done today?

What could I have done better?

What is one way I lived my purpose statement today?

> *If anyone among you thinks he is religious, and does not bridle his tongue but deceives his own heart, this one's religion is useless. Pure and undefiled religion before God and the Father is this: to visit orphans and widows in their trouble, and to keep oneself unspotted from the world.*
> **James 1:26-27**

___ / ___ / ___

Morning

What am I grateful for today?

Who can I pray for or serve this day?

Evening

What good have I done today?

What could I have done better?

What is one way I lived my purpose statement today?

So then each of us shall give account of himself to God.

Romans 14:12

___ / ___ / ___

Morning

What am I grateful for today?

Who can I pray for or serve this day?

Evening

What good have I done today?

What could I have done better?

What is one way I lived my purpose statement today?

The Lord your God in your midst, The Mighty One, will save; He will rejoice over you with gladness, He will quiet you with His love, He will rejoice over you with singing.

Zephaniah 3:17

___ / ___ / ___

Morning

What am I grateful for today?

Who can I pray for or serve this day?

Evening

What good have I done today?

What could I have done better?

What is one way I lived my purpose statement today?

Better is a little with righteousness,
Than vast revenues without justice.

Proverbs 16:8

___ / ___ / ___

Morning

What am I grateful for today?

Who can I pray for or serve this day?

Evening

What good have I done today?

What could I have done better?

What is one way I lived my purpose statement today?

For You are my hope, O Lord God;
You are my trust from my youth.

Psalms 71:5

___ / ___ / ___

Morning

What am I grateful for today?

Who can I pray for or serve this day?

Evening

What good have I done today?

What could I have done better?

What is one way I lived my purpose statement today?

Blessed be the God and Father of our Lord Jesus Christ, who according to His abundant mercy has begotten us again to a living hope through the resurrection of Jesus Christ from the dead.

1 Peter 1:3

___ / ___ / ___

Morning

What am I grateful for today?

Who can I pray for or serve this day?

Evening

What good have I done today?

What could I have done better?

What is one way I lived my purpose statement today?

Hope deferred makes the heart sick,
But when the desire comes, it is a tree of life.

Proverbs 13:12

___ / ___ / ___

Morning

What am I grateful for today?

Who can I pray for or serve this day?

Evening

What good have I done today?

What could I have done better?

What is one way I lived my purpose statement today?

But he who received seed on the good ground is he who hears the word and understands it, who indeed bears fruit and produces: some a hundredfold, some sixty, some thirty.

Matthew 13:23

___ / ___ / ___

Morning

What am I grateful for today?

Who can I pray for or serve this day?

Evening

What good have I done today?

What could I have done better?

What is one way I lived my purpose statement today?

And this I pray, that your love may abound still more and more in knowledge and all discernment.

Philippians 1:9

___ / ___ / ___

Morning

What am I grateful for today?

Who can I pray for or serve this day?

Evening

What good have I done today?

What could I have done better?

What is one way I lived my purpose statement today?

But we all, with unveiled face, beholding as in a mirror the glory of the Lord, are being transformed into the same image from glory to glory, just as by the Spirit of the Lord.

2 Corinthians 3:18

___ / ___ / ___

Morning

What am I grateful for today?

Who can I pray for or serve this day?

Evening

What good have I done today?

What could I have done better?

What is one way I lived my purpose statement today?

*Keep your tongue from evil,
And your lips from speaking deceit.*

Psalms 34:13

___ / ___ / ___

Morning

What am I grateful for today?

Who can I pray for or serve this day?

Evening

What good have I done today?

What could I have done better?

What is one way I lived my purpose statement today?

Wait on the Lord; Be of good courage, And He shall strengthen your heart; Wait, I say, on the Lord!

Psalms 27:14

__ / __ / __

Morning

What am I grateful for today?

Who can I pray for or serve this day?

Evening

What good have I done today?

What could I have done better?

What is one way I lived my purpose statement today?

Be diligent to present yourself approved to God, a worker who does not need to be ashamed, rightly dividing the word of truth.

2 Timothy 2:15

___ / ___ / ___

Morning

What am I grateful for today?

Who can I pray for or serve this day?

Evening

What good have I done today?

What could I have done better?

What is one way I lived my purpose statement today?

*Cast your burden on the Lord, and He shall sustain you;
He shall never permit the righteous to be moved.*

Psalms 55:22

___ / ___ / ___

Morning

What am I grateful for today?

Who can I pray for or serve this day?

Evening

What good have I done today?

What could I have done better?

What is one way I lived my purpose statement today?

Surely he has borne our griefs and carried our sorrows; Yet we esteemed him stricken, smitten by God, and afflicted. But he was wounded for our transgressions, He was crushed for our iniquities; The chastisement for our peace was upon him, And by his stripes we are healed.
Isaiah 53:4-5

___ / ___ / ___

Morning

What am I grateful for today?

Who can I pray for or serve this day?

Evening

What good have I done today?

What could I have done better?

What is one way I lived my purpose statement today?

Now may our Lord Jesus Christ Himself, and our God and Father, who has loved us and given us everlasting consolation and good hope by grace, comfort your hearts and establish you in every good word and work.

2 Thessalonians 2:16, 17

___ / ___ / ___

Morning

What am I grateful for today?

Who can I pray for or serve this day?

Evening

What good have I done today?

What could I have done better?

What is one way I lived my purpose statement today?

Therefore we do not lose heart. Even though our outward man is perishing, yet the inward man is being renewed day by day. For our light affliction, which is but for a moment, is working for us a far more exceeding and eternal weight of glory.

2 Corinthians 4:16, 17

___ / ___ / ___

Morning

What am I grateful for today?

Who can I pray for or serve this day?

Evening

What good have I done today?

What could I have done better?

What is one way I lived my purpose statement today?

All the days of the afflicted are evil, But he who is of a merry heart has a continual feast.

Proverbs 15:15

___ / ___ / ___

Morning

What am I grateful for today?

Who can I pray for or serve this day?

Evening

What good have I done today?

What could I have done better?

What is one way I lived my purpose statement today?

A sound heart is life to the body,
But envy is rottenness to the bones.

Proverbs 14:30

___ / ___ / ___

Morning

What am I grateful for today?

Who can I pray for or serve this day?

Evening

What good have I done today?

What could I have done better?

What is one way I lived my purpose statement today?

Now godliness with contentment is great gain.

1 Timothy 6:6

___ / ___ / ___

Morning

What am I grateful for today?

Who can I pray for or serve this day?

Evening

What good have I done today?

What could I have done better?

What is one way I lived my purpose statement today?

I know how to be abased, and I know how to abound. Everywhere and in all things I have learned both to be full and to be hungry, both to abound and to suffer need. I can do all things through Christ who strengthens me.

Philippians 4:12, 13

___ / ___ / ___

Morning

What am I grateful for today?

Who can I pray for or serve this day?

Evening

What good have I done today?

What could I have done better?

What is one way I lived my purpose statement today?

Do not let your heart envy sinners, But be zealous for the fear of the Lord all the day; For surely there is a hereafter, And your hope will not be cut off.

Proverbs 23:17, 18

___ / ___ / ___

Morning

What am I grateful for today?

Who can I pray for or serve this day?

Evening

What good have I done today?

What could I have done better?

What is one way I lived my purpose statement today?

Come to Me, all you who labor and are heavy laden, and I will give you rest.

Matthew 11:28

___ / ___ / ___

Morning

What am I grateful for today?

Who can I pray for or serve this day?

Evening

What good have I done today?

What could I have done better?

What is one way I lived my purpose statement today?

If a brother or sister is naked and destitute of daily food, and one of you says to them, "Depart in peace, be warmed and filled," but you do not give them the things which are needed for the body, what does it profit?

James 2:15, 16

___ / ___ / ___

Morning

What am I grateful for today?

Who can I pray for or serve this day?

Evening

What good have I done today?

What could I have done better?

What is one way I lived my purpose statement today?

Now may the God of hope fill you with all joy and peace in believing, that you may abound in hope by the power of the Holy Spirit.

Romans 15:13

__ / __ / __

Morning

What am I grateful for today?

Who can I pray for or serve this day?

Evening

What good have I done today?

What could I have done better?

What is one way I lived my purpose statement today?

My little children, these things I write to you, so that you may not sin. And if anyone sins, we have an Advocate with the Father, Jesus Christ the righteous. And He Himself is the propitiation for our sins, and not for ours only but also for the whole world.

1 John 2:1, 2

___ / ___ / ___

Morning

What am I grateful for today?

Who can I pray for or serve this day?

Evening

What good have I done today?

What could I have done better?

What is one way I lived my purpose statement today?

I press toward the goal for the prize of the upward call of God in Christ Jesus. Therefore let us, as many as are mature, have this mind; and if in anything you think otherwise, God will reveal even this to you. Nevertheless, to the degree that we have already attained, let us walk by the same rule, let us be of the same mind.
Philippians 3:14-16

___ / ___ / ___

Morning

What am I grateful for today?

Who can I pray for or serve this day?

Evening

What good have I done today?

What could I have done better?

What is one way I lived my purpose statement today?

For all have sinned and fall short of the glory of God.

___ / ___ / ___

Romans 3:23

Morning

What am I grateful for today?

Who can I pray for or serve this day?

Evening

What good have I done today?

What could I have done better?

What is one way I lived my purpose statement today?

For the Lord loves justice, And does not forsake His saints; They are preserved forever, But the descendants of the wicked shall be cut off.

Psalms 37:28

___ / ___ / ___

Morning

What am I grateful for today?

_____

Who can I pray for or serve this day?

_____

Evening

_____

What good have I done today?

What could I have done better?

_____

What is one way I lived my purpose statement today?

The Lord is my light and my salvation; Whom shall I fear? The Lord is the strength of my life; Of whom shall I be afraid? When the wicked came against me To eat up my flesh, My enemies and foes, They stumbled and fell. Though an army may encamp against me, My heart shall not fear; Though war may rise against me, In this I will be confident.

Psalms 27:1-5

___ / ___ / ___

Morning

What am I grateful for today?

Who can I pray for or serve this day?

Evening

What good have I done today?

What could I have done better?

What is one way I lived my purpose statement today?

Now the Lord is the Spirit; and where the Spirit of the Lord is, there is liberty.

2 Corinthians 3:17

__ / __ / __

Morning

What am I grateful for today?

Who can I pray for or serve this day?

Evening

What good have I done today?

What could I have done better?

What is one way I lived my purpose statement today?

Behold, happy is the man whom God corrects; Therefore do not despise the chastening of the Almighty. For He bruises, but He binds up; He wounds, but His hands make whole.

Job 5:17, 1

___ / ___ / ___

Morning

What am I grateful for today?

Who can I pray for or serve this day?

Evening

What good have I done today?

What could I have done better?

What is one way I lived my purpose statement today?

I will both lie down in peace, and sleep; For You alone, O Lord, make me dwell in safety.

___ / ___ / ___

Psalms 4:8

Morning

What am I grateful for today?

Who can I pray for or serve this day?

Evening

What good have I done today?

What could I have done better?

What is one way I lived my purpose statement today?

Blessed is he who considers the poor; The Lord will deliver him in time of trouble. The Lord will preserve him and keep him alive, And he will be blessed on the earth; You will not deliver him to the will of his enemies.

Psalms 41:1, 2

___ / ___ / ___

Morning

What am I grateful for today?

Who can I pray for or serve this day?

Evening

What good have I done today?

What could I have done better?

What is one way I lived my purpose statement today?

He who has pity on the poor lends to the Lord,
And He will pay back what he has given.

Proverbs 19:17

___ / ___ / ___

Morning

What am I grateful for today?

Who can I pray for or serve this day?

Evening

What good have I done today?

What could I have done better?

What is one way I lived my purpose statement today?

But when you give a feast, invite the poor, the maimed, the lame, the blind. And you will be blessed, because they cannot repay you; for you shall be repaid at the resurrection of the just.

Luke 14:13, 14

___ / ___ / ___

Morning

What am I grateful for today?

Who can I pray for or serve this day?

Evening

What good have I done today?

What could I have done better?

What is one way I lived my purpose statement today?

Then you will understand the fear of the Lord, And find the knowledge of God. For the Lord gives wisdom; From His mouth come knowledge and understanding; He stores up sound wisdom for the upright; He is a shield to those who walk uprightly.

Proverbs 2:5-7

___ / ___ / ___

Morning

What am I grateful for today?

Who can I pray for or serve this day?

Evening

What good have I done today?

What could I have done better?

What is one way I lived my purpose statement today?

*In my distress I cried to the Lord,
and He heard me.*

Psalms 120:1

___ / ___ / ___

Morning

What am I grateful for today?

Who can I pray for or serve this day?

Evening

What good have I done today?

What could I have done better?

What is one way I lived my purpose statement today?

Then Jesus said to His disciples, 'If anyone desires to come after Me, let him deny himself, and take up his cross, and follow Me. For whoever desires to save his life will lose it, but whoever loses his life for My sake will find it. For what profit is it to a man if he gains the whole world, and loses his own soul? Or what will a man give in exchange for his soul?

Matthew 16:24–26

___ / ___ / ___

Morning

What am I grateful for today?

Who can I pray for or serve this day?

Evening

What good have I done today?

What could I have done better?

What is one way I lived my purpose statement today?

The name of the Lord is a strong tower;
The righteous run to it and are safe.

___ / ___ / ___

Proverbs 18:10

Morning

What am I grateful for today?

Who can I pray for or serve this day?

Evening

What good have I done today?

What could I have done better?

What is one way I lived my purpose statement today?

But you, when you pray, go into your room, and when you have shut your door, pray to your Father who is in the secret place; and your Father who sees in secret will reward you openly.

Matthew 6:6

___ / ___ / ___

Morning

What am I grateful for today?

Who can I pray for or serve this day?

Evening

What good have I done today?

What could I have done better?

What is one way I lived my purpose statement today?

*The words of a talebearer are like tasty trifles (wounds),
And they go down into the inmost body.*

Proverbs 18:8

___ / ___ / ___

Morning

What am I grateful for today?

Who can I pray for or serve this day?

Evening

What good have I done today?

What could I have done better?

What is one way I lived my purpose statement today?

You shall laugh at destruction and famine,
And you shall not be afraid of the beasts of the earth.

Job 5:22

___ / ___ / ___

Morning

What am I grateful for today?

Who can I pray for or serve this day?

Evening

What good have I done today?

What could I have done better?

What is one way I lived my purpose statement today?

He will not be afraid of evil tidings;
His heart is steadfast, trusting in the Lord.

___ / ___ / ___

Psalms 112:7

Morning

What am I grateful for today?

Who can I pray for or serve this day?

Evening

What good have I done today?

What could I have done better?

What is one way I lived my purpose statement today?

Because you have made the Lord, who is my refuge, Even the Most High, your dwelling place, No evil shall befall you, Nor shall any plague come near your dwelling.

Psalms 91:9, 10

___ / ___ / ___

Morning

What am I grateful for today?

Who can I pray for or serve this day?

Evening

What good have I done today?

What could I have done better?

What is one way I lived my purpose statement today?

> ...Fear not, for I have redeemed you; I have called you by your name; You are Mine. When you pass through the waters, I will be with you; And through the rivers, they shall not overflow you. When you walk through the fire, you shall not be burned, Nor shall the flame scorch you.
>
> **Isaiah 43:1, 2**

___ / ___ / ___

Morning

What am I grateful for today?

Who can I pray for or serve this day?

Evening

What good have I done today?

What could I have done better?

What is one way I lived my purpose statement today?

He who despises his neighbor sins;
But he who has mercy on the poor, happy is he.

Proverbs 14:21

___ / ___ / ___

Morning

What am I grateful for today?

Who can I pray for or serve this day?

Evening

What good have I done today?

What could I have done better?

What is one way I lived my purpose statement today?

For we walk by faith, not by sight.

___ / ___ / ___

2 Corinthians 5:7

Morning

What am I grateful for today?

Who can I pray for or serve this day?

Evening

What good have I done today?

What could I have done better?

What is one way I lived my purpose statement today?

For assuredly, I say to you, whoever says to this mountain, 'Be removed and be cast into the sea,' and does not doubt in his heart, but believes that those things he says will be done, he will have whatever he says. Therefore I say to you, whatever things you ask when you pray, believe that you receive them, and you will have them.
Mark 11:23, 24

___ / ___ / ___

Morning

What am I grateful for today?

Who can I pray for or serve this day?

Evening

What good have I done today?

What could I have done better?

What is one way I lived my purpose statement today?

And that from childhood you have known the Holy Scriptures, which are able to make you wise for salvation through faith which is in Christ Jesus. All Scripture is given by inspiration of God, and is profitable for doctrine, for reproof, for correction, for instruction in righteousness.

2 Timothy 3:15, 16

___ / ___ / ___

Morning

What am I grateful for today?

Who can I pray for or serve this day?

Evening

What good have I done today?

What could I have done better?

What is one way I lived my purpose statement today?

But without faith it is impossible to please Him, for he who comes to God must believe that He is, and that He is a rewarder of those who diligently seek Him.

Hebrews 11:6

___ / ___ / ___

Morning

What am I grateful for today?

Who can I pray for or serve this day?

Evening

What good have I done today?

What could I have done better?

What is one way I lived my purpose statement today?

In all your ways acknowledge Him,
And He shall direct your paths.

___ / ___ / ___

Proverbs 3:6

Morning

What am I grateful for today?

Who can I pray for or serve this day?

Evening

What good have I done today?

What could I have done better?

What is one way I lived my purpose statement today?

But the very hairs of your head are all numbered. Do not fear therefore; you are of more value than many sparrows.

Luke 12:7

___ / ___ / ___

Morning

What am I grateful for today?

Who can I pray for or serve this day?

Evening

What good have I done today?

What could I have done better?

What is one way I lived my purpose statement today?

If any of you lacks wisdom, let him ask of God, who gives to all liberally and without reproach, and it will be given to him. But let him ask in faith, with no doubting, for he who doubts is like a wave of the sea driven and tossed by the wind.

James 1:5, 6

___ / ___ / ___

Morning

What am I grateful for today?

Who can I pray for or serve this day?

Evening

What good have I done today?

What could I have done better?

What is one way I lived my purpose statement today?

So then faith comes by hearing, and hearing by the word of God.

Romans 10:17

___ / ___ / ___

Morning

What am I grateful for today?

Who can I pray for or serve this day?

Evening

What good have I done today?

What could I have done better?

What is one way I lived my purpose statement today?

God is our refuge and strength, A very present help in trouble. Therefore we will not fear, Even though the earth be removed, And though the mountains be carried into the midst of the sea.

Psalms 46:1, 2

___ / ___ / ___

Morning

What am I grateful for today?

Who can I pray for or serve this day?

Evening

What good have I done today?

What could I have done better?

What is one way I lived my purpose statement today?

As you therefore have received Christ Jesus the Lord, so walk in Him, rooted and built up in Him and established in the faith, as you have been taught, abounding in it with thanksgiving.

Colossians 2:6, 7

___ / ___ / ___

Morning

What am I grateful for today?

Who can I pray for or serve this day?

Evening

What good have I done today?

What could I have done better?

What is one way I lived my purpose statement today?

For by grace you have been saved through faith, and that not of yourselves; it is the gift of God.

Ephesians 2:8

___ / ___ / ___

Morning

What am I grateful for today?

Who can I pray for or serve this day?

Evening

What good have I done today?

What could I have done better?

What is one way I lived my purpose statement today?

For you are all sons of God through faith in Christ Jesus.

___ / ___ / ___

Galatians 3:26

Morning

What am I grateful for today?

Who can I pray for or serve this day?

Evening

What good have I done today?

What could I have done better?

What is one way I lived my purpose statement today?

As each one has received a gift, minister it to one another, as good stewards of the manifold grace of God.

1 Peter 4:10

___ / ___ / ___

Morning

What am I grateful for today?

Who can I pray for or serve this day?

Evening

What good have I done today?

What could I have done better?

What is one way I lived my purpose statement today?

Have I not commanded you? Be strong and of good courage; do not be afraid, nor be dismayed, for the Lord your God is with you wherever you go.

Joshua 1:9

___ / ___ / ___

Morning

What am I grateful for today?

Who can I pray for or serve this day?

Evening

What good have I done today?

What could I have done better?

What is one way I lived my purpose statement today?

Watch, stand fast in the faith, be brave, be strong..

___ / ___ / ___

1 Corinthians 16:13

Morning

What am I grateful for today?

Who can I pray for or serve this day?

Evening

What good have I done today?

What could I have done better?

What is one way I lived my purpose statement today?

But the fruit of the Spirit is love, joy, peace, longsuffering, kindness, goodness, faithfulness.

Galatians 5:22

___ / ___ / ___

Morning

What am I grateful for today?

Who can I pray for or serve this day?

Evening

What good have I done today?

What could I have done better?

What is one way I lived my purpose statement today?

I have been crucified with Christ; it is no longer I who live, but Christ lives in me; and the life which I now live in the flesh I live by faith in the Son of God, who loved me and gave Himself for me.

Galatians 2:20

___ / ___ / ___

Morning

What am I grateful for today?

Who can I pray for or serve this day?

Evening

What good have I done today?

What could I have done better?

What is one way I lived my purpose statement today?

Therefore, as the elect of God, holy and beloved, put on tender mercies, kindness, humility, meekness, longsuffering;

Colossians 3:12

__ / __ / __

Morning

What am I grateful for today?

Who can I pray for or serve this day?

Evening

What good have I done today?

What could I have done better?

What is one way I lived my purpose statement today?

A soft answer turns away wrath, but a harsh word stirs up anger.

Proverbs 15:1

___ / ___ / ___

Morning

What am I grateful for today?

Who can I pray for or serve this day?

Evening

What good have I done today?

What could I have done better?

What is one way I lived my purpose statement today?

Lord, make me to know my end, And what is the measure of my days, That I may know how frail I am. Indeed, You have made my days as handbreadths, And my age is as nothing before You; Certainly every man at his best state is but vapor.

Psalms 39:4, 5

__ / __ / __

Morning

What am I grateful for today?

Who can I pray for or serve this day?

Evening

What good have I done today?

What could I have done better?

What is one way I lived my purpose statement today?

But those who wait on the Lord shall renew their strength; they shall mount up with wings like eagles, they shall run and not be weary, they shall walk and not faint.

Isaiah 40:31

___ / ___ / ___

Morning

What am I grateful for today?

Who can I pray for or serve this day?

Evening

What good have I done today?

What could I have done better?

What is one way I lived my purpose statement today?

For I was hungry and you gave Me food; I was thirsty and you gave Me drink; I was a stranger and you took Me in; I was naked and you clothed Me; I was sick and you visited Me; I was in prison and you came to Me.

Matthew 25:35, 36

___ / ___ / ___

Morning

What am I grateful for today?

Who can I pray for or serve this day?

Evening

What good have I done today?

What could I have done better?

What is one way I lived my purpose statement today?

Do not forget to entertain strangers, for by so doing some have unwittingly entertained angels.

Hebrews 13:2

__ / __ / __

Morning

What am I grateful for today?

Who can I pray for or serve this day?

Evening

What good have I done today?

What could I have done better?

What is one way I lived my purpose statement today?

For whoever gives you a cup of water to drink in My name, because you belong to Christ, assuredly, I say to you, he will by no means lose his reward.

Mark 9:41

___ / ___ / ___

Morning

What am I grateful for today?

Who can I pray for or serve this day?

Evening

What good have I done today?

What could I have done better?

What is one way I lived my purpose statement today?

> *That Christ may dwell in your hearts through faith; that you, being rooted and grounded in love, may be able to comprehend with all the saints what is the width and length and depth and height - to know the love of Christ which passes knowledge; that you may be filled with all the fullness of God.*
> **Ephesians 3:17-19**

___ / ___ / ___

Morning

What am I grateful for today?

Who can I pray for or serve this day?

Evening

What good have I done today?

What could I have done better?

What is one way I lived my purpose statement today?

> *Yet in all these things we are more than conquerors through Him who loved us. For I am persuaded that neither death nor life, nor angels nor principalities nor powers, nor things present nor things to come, nor height nor depth, nor any other created thing, shall be able to separate us from the love of God which is in Christ Jesus our Lord.*
> **Romans 8:37-39**

___ / ___ / ___

Morning

What am I grateful for today?

Who can I pray for or serve this day?

Evening

What good have I done today?

What could I have done better?

What is one way I lived my purpose statement today?

In the day of my trouble I will call upon You, for You will answer me.

___ / ___ / ___

Psalm 86:7

Morning

What am I grateful for today?

Who can I pray for or serve this day?

Evening

What good have I done today?

What could I have done better?

What is one way I lived my purpose statement today?

Though an army may encamp against me, My heart shall not fear; Though war may rise against me, In this I will be confident.

Psalms 27:3

___ / ___ / ___

Morning

What am I grateful for today?

Who can I pray for or serve this day?

Evening

What good have I done today?

What could I have done better?

What is one way I lived my purpose statement today?

For I, the Lord your God, will hold your right hand,
Saying to you, 'Fear not, I will help you.'

Isaiah 41:13

___ / ___ / ___

Morning

What am I grateful for today?

Who can I pray for or serve this day?

Evening

What good have I done today?

What could I have done better?

What is one way I lived my purpose statement today?

But whoever listens to me will dwell safely,
And will be secure, without fear of evil.

Proverbs 1:33

___ / ___ / ___

Morning

What am I grateful for today?

Who can I pray for or serve this day?

Evening

What good have I done today?

What could I have done better?

What is one way I lived my purpose statement today?

Fear not, for I am with you; Be not dismayed, for I am your God. I will strengthen you, Yes, I will help you, I will uphold you with My righteous right hand.

Isaiah 41:10

___ / ___ / ___

Morning

What am I grateful for today?

Who can I pray for or serve this day?

Evening

What good have I done today?

What could I have done better?

What is one way I lived my purpose statement today?

But God, who is rich in mercy, because of His great love with which He loved us, even when we were dead in trespasses, made us alive together with Christ (by grace you have been saved), and raised us up together, and made us sit together in the heavenly places in Christ Jesus, that in the ages to come He might show the exceeding riches of His grace in His kindness toward us in Christ Jesus.
Ephesians 2:4-7

___ / ___ / ___

Morning

What am I grateful for today?

Who can I pray for or serve this day?

Evening

What good have I done today?

What could I have done better?

What is one way I lived my purpose statement today?

And do not fear those who kill the body but cannot kill the soul. But rather fear Him who is able to destroy both soul and body in hell.

Matthew 10:28

___ / ___ / ___

Morning

What am I grateful for today?

Who can I pray for or serve this day?

Evening

What good have I done today?

What could I have done better?

What is one way I lived my purpose statement today?

Do not be afraid of sudden terror, Nor of trouble from the wicked when it comes; For the Lord will be your confidence, And will keep your foot from being caught.

Proverbs 3:25, 26

___ / ___ / ___

Morning

What am I grateful for today?

Who can I pray for or serve this day?

Evening

What good have I done today?

What could I have done better?

What is one way I lived my purpose statement today?

Bears all things, believes all things, hopes all things, endures all things. Love never fails. But whether there are prophecies, they will fail; whether there are tongues, they will cease; whether there is knowledge, it will vanish away.

1 Corinthians 13:7-8

___ / ___ / ___

Morning

What am I grateful for today?

Who can I pray for or serve this day?

Evening

What good have I done today?

What could I have done better?

What is one way I lived my purpose statement today?

For this is God, Our God forever and ever;
He will be our guide Even to death.

___ / ___ / ___

Psalms 48:14

Morning

What am I grateful for today?

Who can I pray for or serve this day?

Evening

What good have I done today?

What could I have done better?

What is one way I lived my purpose statement today?

A man's heart plans his way, But the Lord directs his steps.

Proverbs 16:9

___ / ___ / ___

Morning

What am I grateful for today?

Who can I pray for or serve this day?

Evening

What good have I done today?

What could I have done better?

What is one way I lived my purpose statement today?

*The steps of a good man are ordered by the Lord,
And He delights in his way.*

Psalms 37:23

___ / ___ / ___

Morning

What am I grateful for today?

Who can I pray for or serve this day?

Evening

What good have I done today?

What could I have done better?

What is one way I lived my purpose statement today?

It shall come to pass in the day the Lord gives you rest from your sorrow, and from your fear and the hard bondage in which you were made to serve.

Isaiah 14:3

___ / ___ / ___

Morning

What am I grateful for today?

Who can I pray for or serve this day?

Evening

What good have I done today?

What could I have done better?

What is one way I lived my purpose statement today?

When you lie down, you will not be afraid; Yes, you will lie down and your sleep will be sweet.

___ / ___ / ___

Proverbs 3:24

Morning

What am I grateful for today?

Who can I pray for or serve this day?

Evening

What good have I done today?

What could I have done better?

What is one way I lived my purpose statement today?

For the eyes of the Lord are on the righteous, And His ears are open to their prayers; But the face of the Lord is against those who do evil. And who is he who will harm you if you become followers of what is good? But even if you should suffer for righteousness' sake, you are blessed. And do not be afraid of their threats, nor be troubled.
1 Peter 3:12-14

___ / ___ / ___

Morning

What am I grateful for today?

Who can I pray for or serve this day?

Evening

What good have I done today?

What could I have done better?

What is one way I lived my purpose statement today?

So let each one give as he purposes in his heart, not grudgingly or of necessity; for God loves a cheerful giver.

2 Corinthians 9:7

___ / ___ / ___

Morning

What am I grateful for today?

Who can I pray for or serve this day?

Evening

What good have I done today?

What could I have done better?

What is one way I lived my purpose statement today?

In righteousness you shall be established; You shall be far from oppression, for you shall not fear; And from terror, for it shall not come near you.

Isaiah 54:14

___ / ___ / ___

Morning

What am I grateful for today?

Who can I pray for or serve this day?

Evening

What good have I done today?

What could I have done better?

What is one way I lived my purpose statement today?

So we may boldly say: 'The Lord is my helper; I will not fear. What can man do to me?'

Hebrews 13:6

___ / ___ / ___

Morning

What am I grateful for today?

Who can I pray for or serve this day?

Evening

What good have I done today?

What could I have done better?

What is one way I lived my purpose statement today?

Your word I have hidden in my heart, that I might not sin against You.

Psalms 119:11

___ / ___ / ___

Morning

What am I grateful for today?

Who can I pray for or serve this day?

Evening

What good have I done today?

What could I have done better?

What is one way I lived my purpose statement today?

I will bring the blind by a way they did not know; I will lead them in paths they have not known. I will make darkness light before them, And crooked places straight. These things I will do for them, And not forsake them.

Isaiah 42:16

___ / ___ / ___

Morning

What am I grateful for today?

Who can I pray for or serve this day?

Evening

What good have I done today?

What could I have done better?

What is one way I lived my purpose statement today?

For it is the God who commanded light to shine out of darkness, who has shone in our hearts to give the light of the knowledge of the glory of God in the face of Jesus Christ.

2 Corinthians 4:6

___ / ___ / ___

Morning

What am I grateful for today?

Who can I pray for or serve this day?

Evening

What good have I done today?

What could I have done better?

What is one way I lived my purpose statement today?

In My Father's house are many mansions; if it were not so, I would have told you. I go to prepare a place for you. And if I go and prepare a place for you, I will come again and receive you to Myself; that where I am, there you may be also.

John 14:2, 3

___ / ___ / ___

Morning

What am I grateful for today?

Who can I pray for or serve this day?

Evening

What good have I done today?

What could I have done better?

What is one way I lived my purpose statement today?

The fear of man brings a snare,
But whoever trusts in the Lord shall be safe.

Proverbs 29:25

___ / ___ / ___

Morning

What am I grateful for today?

Who can I pray for or serve this day?

Evening

What good have I done today?

What could I have done better?

What is one way I lived my purpose statement today?

He shall cover you with His feathers, And under His wings you shall take refuge; His truth shall be your shield and buckler. You shall not be afraid of the terror by night, Nor of the arrow that flies by day, Nor of the pestilence that walks in darkness, Nor of the destruction that lays waste at noonday.
Psalms 91:4-6

__ / __ / __

Morning

What am I grateful for today?

Who can I pray for or serve this day?

Evening

What good have I done today?

What could I have done better?

What is one way I lived my purpose statement today?

Do not fear, for you will not be ashamed; Neither be disgraced, for you will not be put to shame; For you will forget the shame of your youth, And will not remember the reproach of your widowhood anymore.

Isaiah 54:4

___ / ___ / ___

Morning

What am I grateful for today?

Who can I pray for or serve this day?

Evening

What good have I done today?

What could I have done better?

What is one way I lived my purpose statement today?

But Jesus looked at them and said, 'With men it is impossible, but not with God; for with God all things are possible.

Mark 10:27

__ / __ / __

Morning

What am I grateful for today?

Who can I pray for or serve this day?

Evening

What good have I done today?

What could I have done better?

What is one way I lived my purpose statement today?

Humble yourselves in the sight of the Lord, and He will lift you up.

___ / ___ / ___

James 4:10

Morning

What am I grateful for today?

Who can I pray for or serve this day?

Evening

What good have I done today?

What could I have done better?

What is one way I lived my purpose statement today?

Jesus said to her, 'I am the resurrection and the life. He who believes in Me, though he may die, he shall live. And whoever lives and believes in Me shall never die. Do you believe this?'

John 11:25, 26

___ / ___ / ___

Morning

What am I grateful for today?

Who can I pray for or serve this day?

Evening

What good have I done today?

What could I have done better?

What is one way I lived my purpose statement today?

The Lord is my rock and my fortress and my deliverer; My God, my strength, in whom I will trust; My shield and the horn of my salvation, my stronghold.

Psalms 18:2

___ / ___ / ___

Morning

What am I grateful for today?

Who can I pray for or serve this day?

Evening

What good have I done today?

What could I have done better?

What is one way I lived my purpose statement today?

He shall be like a tree Planted by the rivers of water, That brings forth its fruit in its season, Whose leaf also shall not wither; And whatever he does shall prosper.

Psalms 1:3

___ / ___ / ___

Morning

What am I grateful for today?

Who can I pray for or serve this day?

Evening

What good have I done today?

What could I have done better?

What is one way I lived my purpose statement today?

You shall not steal, nor deal falsely, nor lie to one another.

___ / ___ / ___

Leviticus 19:11

Morning

What am I grateful for today?

Who can I pray for or serve this day?

Evening

What good have I done today?

What could I have done better?

What is one way I lived my purpose statement today?

Dishonest scales are an abomination to the Lord,
But a just weight is His delight.

Proverbs 11:1

___ / ___ / ___

Morning

What am I grateful for today?

Who can I pray for or serve this day?

Evening

What good have I done today?

What could I have done better?

What is one way I lived my purpose statement today?

Even to your old age, I am He, And even to gray hairs I will carry you! I have made, and I will bear; Even I will carry, and will deliver you.

Isaiah 46:4

___ / ___ / ___

Morning

What am I grateful for today?

Who can I pray for or serve this day?

Evening

What good have I done today?

What could I have done better?

What is one way I lived my purpose statement today?

> *Likewise the Spirit also helps in our weaknesses. For we do not know what we should pray for as we ought, but the Spirit Himself makes intercession for us with groanings which cannot be uttered. Now He who searches the hearts knows what the mind of the Spirit is, because He makes intercession for the saints according to the will of God.*
> **Romans 8:26, 27**

__ / __ / __

Morning

What am I grateful for today?

Who can I pray for or serve this day?

Evening

What good have I done today?

What could I have done better?

What is one way I lived my purpose statement today?

He who has a generous eye will be blessed,
For he gives of his bread to the poor.

Proverbs 22:9

___ / ___ / ___

Morning

What am I grateful for today?

Who can I pray for or serve this day?

Evening

What good have I done today?

What could I have done better?

What is one way I lived my purpose statement today?

Jesus said to him, 'You shall love the Lord your God with all your heart, with all your soul, and with all your mind.' This is the first and great commandment. And the second is like it: 'You shall love your neighbor as yourself.'

Matthew 22:37–39

___ / ___ / ___

Morning

What am I grateful for today?

Who can I pray for or serve this day?

Evening

What good have I done today?

What could I have done better?

What is one way I lived my purpose statement today?

Therefore I say to you, her sins, which are many, are forgiven, for she loved much. But to whom little is forgiven, the same loves little.

Luke 7:47

___ / ___ / ___

Morning

What am I grateful for today?

Who can I pray for or serve this day?

Evening

What good have I done today?

What could I have done better?

What is one way I lived my purpose statement today?

Love suffers long and is kind; love does not parade itself, is not puffed up; does not behave rudely, does not seek its own, is not provoked, thinks no evil; does not rejoice in iniquity, but rejoices in the truth; bears all things, believes all things, hopes all things, endures all things.
1 Corinthians 13:4–7

___ / ___ / ___

Morning

What am I grateful for today?

Who can I pray for or serve this day?

Evening

What good have I done today?

What could I have done better?

What is one way I lived my purpose statement today?

There is no fear in love; but perfect love casts out fear, because fear involves torment. But he who fears has not been made perfect in love.

1 John 4:18

___ / ___ / ___

Morning

What am I grateful for today?

Who can I pray for or serve this day?

Evening

What good have I done today?

What could I have done better?

What is one way I lived my purpose statement today?

We love Him because He first loved us.

___ / ___ / ___

1 John 4:19

Morning

What am I grateful for today?

Who can I pray for or serve this day?

Evening

What good have I done today?

What could I have done better?

What is one way I lived my purpose statement today?

I will not leave you orphans; I will come to you.

___ / ___ / ___

John 14:18

Morning

What am I grateful for today?

Who can I pray for or serve this day?

Evening

What good have I done today?

What could I have done better?

What is one way I lived my purpose statement today?

> *Whom having not seen you love. Though now you do not see Him, yet believing, you rejoice with joy inexpressible and full of glory.*
>
> **1 Peter 1:8**

___ / ___ / ___

Morning

What am I grateful for today?

Who can I pray for or serve this day?

Evening

What good have I done today?

What could I have done better?

What is one way I lived my purpose statement today?

But whoever has this world's goods, and sees his brother in need, and shuts up his heart from him, how does the love of God abide in him?

1 John 3:17T

___ / ___ / ___

Morning

What am I grateful for today?

Who can I pray for or serve this day?

Evening

What good have I done today?

What could I have done better?

What is one way I lived my purpose statement today?

Then he said to them, 'Go your way, eat the fat, drink the sweet, and send portions to those for whom nothing is prepared; for this day is holy to our Lord. Do not sorrow, for the joy of the Lord is your strength.'

Nehemiah 8:10

___ / ___ / ___

Morning

What am I grateful for today?

Who can I pray for or serve this day?

Evening

What good have I done today?

What could I have done better?

What is one way I lived my purpose statement today?

*A friend loves at all times,
and a brother is born for adversity.*

Proverbs 17:17

__ / __ / __

Morning

What am I grateful for today?

Who can I pray for or serve this day?

Evening

What good have I done today?

What could I have done better?

What is one way I lived my purpose statement today?

Give, and it will be given to you: good measure, pressed down, shaken together, and running over will be put into your bosom. For with the same measure that you use, it will be measured back to you.

Luke 6:38

___ / ___ / ___

Morning

What am I grateful for today?

Who can I pray for or serve this day?

Evening

What good have I done today?

What could I have done better?

What is one way I lived my purpose statement today?

Be strong and of good courage, do not fear nor be afraid of them; for the Lord your God, He is the One who goes with you. He will not leave you nor forsake you.

Deuteronomy 31:6

___ / ___ / ___

Morning

What am I grateful for today?

Who can I pray for or serve this day?

Evening

What good have I done today?

What could I have done better?

What is one way I lived my purpose statement today?

Peace I leave with you, My peace I give to you; not as the world gives do I give to you. Let not your heart be troubled, neither let it be afraid.

John 14:27

__ / __ / __

Morning

What am I grateful for today?

Who can I pray for or serve this day?

Evening

What good have I done today?

What could I have done better?

What is one way I lived my purpose statement today?

Yea, though I walk through the valley of the shadow of death, I will fear no evil; For You are with me; Your rod and Your staff, they comfort me. You prepare a table before me in the presence of my enemies; You anoint my head with oil; My cup runs over.

Psalms 23:4, 5

___ / ___ / ___

Morning

What am I grateful for today?

Who can I pray for or serve this day?

Evening

What good have I done today?

What could I have done better?

What is one way I lived my purpose statement today?

> *But I say to you, love your enemies, bless those who curse you, do good to those who hate you, and pray for those who spitefully use you and persecute you, that you may be sons of your Father in heaven; for He makes His sun rise on the evil and on the good, and sends rain on the just and on the unjust.*
> **Matthew 5:44, 45**

___ / ___ / ___

Morning

What am I grateful for today?

Who can I pray for or serve this day?

Evening

What good have I done today?

What could I have done better?

What is one way I lived my purpose statement today?

If we confess our sins, He is faithful and just to forgive us our sins and to cleanse us from all unrighteousness.

1 John 1:9

___ / ___ / ___

Morning

What am I grateful for today?

Who can I pray for or serve this day?

Evening

What good have I done today?

What could I have done better?

What is one way I lived my purpose statement today?

For if you forgive men their trespasses,
your heavenly Father will also forgive you.

Matthew 6:14

__ / __ / __

Morning

What am I grateful for today?

Who can I pray for or serve this day?

Evening

What good have I done today?

What could I have done better?

What is one way I lived my purpose statement today?

Therefore 'If your enemy is hungry, feed him; If he is thirsty, give him a drink; For in so doing you will heap coals of fire on his head.'

Romans 12:20

___ / ___ / ___

Morning

What am I grateful for today?

Who can I pray for or serve this day?

Evening

What good have I done today?

What could I have done better?

What is one way I lived my purpose statement today?

So he answered, 'Do not fear, for those who are with us are more than those who are with them.'

2 Kings 6:16

___ / ___ / ___

Morning

What am I grateful for today?

Who can I pray for or serve this day?

Evening

What good have I done today?

What could I have done better?

What is one way I lived my purpose statement today?

These things I have spoken to you, that in Me you may have peace. In the world you will have tribulation; but be of good cheer, I have overcome the world.

John 16:33

___ / ___ / ___

Morning

What am I grateful for today?

Who can I pray for or serve this day?

Evening

What good have I done today?

What could I have done better?

What is one way I lived my purpose statement today?

Greater love has no one than this, than to lay down one's life for his friends.

John 15:13

___ / ___ / ___

Morning

What am I grateful for today?

Who can I pray for or serve this day?

Evening

What good have I done today?

What could I have done better?

What is one way I lived my purpose statement today?

But the salvation of the righteous is from the Lord;
He is their strength in the time of trouble.

Psalms 37:39

__ / __ / __

Morning

What am I grateful for today?

Who can I pray for or serve this day?

Evening

What good have I done today?

What could I have done better?

What is one way I lived my purpose statement today?

The Lord opens the eyes of the blind; The Lord raises those who are bowed down; The Lord loves the righteous.

Psalms 146:8

___ / ___ / ___

Morning

What am I grateful for today?

Who can I pray for or serve this day?

Evening

What good have I done today?

What could I have done better?

What is one way I lived my purpose statement today?

And we know that all things work together for good to those who love God, to those who are the called according to His purpose.

Romans 8:28

___ / ___ / ___

Morning

What am I grateful for today?

Who can I pray for or serve this day?

Evening

What good have I done today?

What could I have done better?

What is one way I lived my purpose statement today?

Owe no one anything except to love one another, for he who loves another has fulfilled the law.

Romans 13:8

___ / ___ / ___

Morning

What am I grateful for today?

Who can I pray for or serve this day?

Evening

What good have I done today?

What could I have done better?

What is one way I lived my purpose statement today?

For God has not given us a spirit of fear,
but of power and of love and of a sound mind.

2 Timothy 1:7

___ / ___ / ___

Morning

What am I grateful for today?

Who can I pray for or serve this day?

Evening

What good have I done today?

What could I have done better?

What is one way I lived my purpose statement today?

Where there is no wood, the fire goes out; And where there is no talebearer, strife ceases. As charcoal is to burning coals, and wood to fire, So is a contentious man to kindle strife.

Proverbs 26:20, 21

___ / ___ / ___

Morning

What am I grateful for today?

Who can I pray for or serve this day?

Evening

What good have I done today?

What could I have done better?

What is one way I lived my purpose statement today?

*The Lord is good, A stronghold in the day of trouble;
And He knows those who trust in Him.*

Nahum 1:7

__ / __ / __

Morning

What am I grateful for today?

Who can I pray for or serve this day?

Evening

What good have I done today?

What could I have done better?

What is one way I lived my purpose statement today?

Do not lie to one another, since you have put off the old man with his deeds, and have put on the new man who is renewed in knowledge according to the image of Him who created him.

Colossians 3:9, 10

___ / ___ / ___

Morning

What am I grateful for today?

Who can I pray for or serve this day?

Evening

What good have I done today?

What could I have done better?

What is one way I lived my purpose statement today?

Do not withhold good from those to whom it is due When it is in the power of your hand to do so.

Proverbs 3:27

___ / ___ / ___

Morning

What am I grateful for today?

Who can I pray for or serve this day?

Evening

What good have I done today?

What could I have done better?

What is one way I lived my purpose statement today?

My brethren, count it all joy when you fall into various trials, knowing that the testing of your faith produces patience. But let patience have its perfect work, that you may be perfect and complete, lacking nothing.

James 1:2-4

___ / ___ / ___

Morning

What am I grateful for today?

Who can I pray for or serve this day?

Evening

What good have I done today?

What could I have done better?

What is one way I lived my purpose statement today?

"ou are my hiding place; You shall preserve me from trouble; You shall surround me with songs of deliverance.

Psalms 32:7

___ / ___ / ___

Morning

What am I grateful for today?

Who can I pray for or serve this day?

Evening

What good have I done today?

What could I have done better?

What is one way I lived my purpose statement today?

Having been born again, not of corruptible seed but incorruptible, through the word of God which lives and abides forever.

1 Peter 1:23

___ / ___ / ___

Morning

What am I grateful for today?

Who can I pray for or serve this day?

Evening

What good have I done today?

What could I have done better?

What is one way I lived my purpose statement today?

Do not be deceived, my beloved brethren. Every good gift and every perfect gift is from above, and comes down from the Father of lights, with whom there is no variation or shadow of turning.

James 1:16-17

___ / ___ / ___

Morning

What am I grateful for today?

Who can I pray for or serve this day?

Evening

What good have I done today?

What could I have done better?

What is one way I lived my purpose statement today?

Delight yourself also in the Lord,
And He shall give you the desires of your heart.

Psalms 37:4

___ / ___ / ___

Morning

What am I grateful for today?

Who can I pray for or serve this day?

Evening

What good have I done today?

What could I have done better?

What is one way I lived my purpose statement today?

But as it is written: 'Eye has not seen, nor ear heard, Nor have entered into the heart of man The things which God has prepared for those who love Him.'

1 Corinthians 2:9

___ / ___ / ___

Morning

What am I grateful for today?

Who can I pray for or serve this day?

Evening

What good have I done today?

What could I have done better?

What is one way I lived my purpose statement today?

Why are you cast down, O my soul? And why are you disquieted within me? Hope in God; For I shall yet praise Him, The help of my countenance and my God.

Psalms 42:11

___ / ___ / ___

Morning

What am I grateful for today?

Who can I pray for or serve this day?

Evening

What good have I done today?

What could I have done better?

What is one way I lived my purpose statement today?

He who is slow to anger is better than the mighty, and he who rules his spirit than he who takes a city.

Proverbs 16:32

___ / ___ / ___

Morning

What am I grateful for today?

Who can I pray for or serve this day?

Evening

What good have I done today?

What could I have done better?

What is one way I lived my purpose statement today?

And God will wipe away every tear from their eyes; there shall be no more death, nor sorrow, nor crying. There shall be no more pain, for the former things have passed away.

Revelation 21:4

___ / ___ / ___

Morning

What am I grateful for today?

Who can I pray for or serve this day?

Evening

What good have I done today?

What could I have done better?

What is one way I lived my purpose statement today?

And I commend joy, for man has nothing better under the sun but to eat and drink and be joyful, for this will go with him in his toil through the days of his life that God has given him under the sun.

Ecclesiastes 8:15

___ / ___ / ___

Morning

What am I grateful for today?

Who can I pray for or serve this day?

Evening

What good have I done today?

What could I have done better?

What is one way I lived my purpose statement today?

My son, do not forget my law, But let your heart keep my commands; For length of days and long life And peace they will add to you.

Proverbs 3:1, 2

___ / ___ / ___

Morning

What am I grateful for today?

Who can I pray for or serve this day?

Evening

What good have I done today?

What could I have done better?

What is one way I lived my purpose statement today?

Congratulations!

You have just finished six months' of your Spiritual Disciplines Journal! You've moved through days where it may have been difficult to resist the urge to grab your phone and start your busy day, and to instead, to close your eyes and pray, then pick up the pen and write. Perhaps you have caught yourself leaping out of bed to tackle a busy day, and then remembered at the last minute to lay back down to complete your reading, journaling and prayer. Perhaps you forgot to complete your journaling on evenings where you were already cozy in bed and closing your eyes, and suddenly remembered you hadn't yet read or prayed or filled in your journal that day. Yet you took the time to do it. All through the grace of God and your commitment to caring for your spirit, loving others and loving God.

Now is the time to take a deep breath, smile and rest a few moments to celebrate. These moments allow us to take stock of the past and, trusting in God, to plan for the future. Please enjoy this moment by treating yourself to something nice. How has the Spiritual Disciplines Journal changed your life, your connection to others and to God, your attitude or your spiritual growth? We'd love to hear your story! Email us at **hello@spiritualdisciplinesjournal.com**. You can also get yourself, or others who want to share your discovery with, a brand new copy of the journal at **SpiritualDisciplinesJournal.com** so you can continue your spiritual growth tomorrow.

In Conclusion

I'm overjoyed and, of course, grateful to be able to share this journal with you! If you want more journals for yourself, friends, family or loved ones, you can visit **SpiritualDisciplinesJournal.com**, where you can also find more information about the science and the practice of gratitude.

In addition, a perfect companion book to this journal is my book *Fit Soul: Tools, Tactics & Habits For Optimizing Spiritual Fitness*, which is available as a free download or inexpensive hard copy at FitSoulBook.com. Within the pages of Fit Soul, you'll find even more tips and directions for weaving the spiritual disciplines into your life!

In Him,

Ben Greenfield